Insomnia

EDWARD VIDAURRE

McAllen, Texas

Copyright © 2014 Edward Vidaurre
All rights reserved. No part of this book may be transmitted or reproduced in any form or by any electronic or mechanical means, including information retrieval systems, without permission in writing from the publisher, except by a reviewer who may quote brief passages in printed reviews.

Published by El Zarape Press: McAllen, Texas.

Insomnia by Edward Vidaurre
Introduction by Katherine Hoerth
Edited by Daniel García Ordaz

ISBN-13: 978-1499525793
ISBN-10: 1499525796

Poetry

Cover design by Edward Vidaurre, Ileana García-Spitz, and Daniel García Ordaz.
Cover photographs and illustration by Ileana García-Spitz.

Printed in the United States of America.

DEDICATION

for
Bella Vidaurre
who sleeps and dreams
a little dream for me

CONTENTS

Acknowledgements 5
Introduction by Katherine Hoerth 6
Part One: Night 8
    Sleep Apnea 9
    Submerged 10
    The Well 11
    Siesta Haikus 12
    Resaca Dreams 13
    Our First Song 14
    Pantoum Dream 15
    At Your Front Door 16
    In a Brief Instance, She Vanished . . . 17
    My Poetise Incognito 18
    When The Soul Sleeps 19
    Absence Of Light 20
    Night 21
    I Lost My Soul In The River Styx That Flows . . . 22
Part Two: Morning 23
    Fragments 24
    How Quickly The Leaves Razor Over The Heads . . . 25
    My Darling Son, My Warm Heart 26
    Unrequited Love, a sestina 27
    The Recliner 29
    Forgotten Man 30
    Edible Earth 31
    Conversations With My Greñuda 33
    How to watch me wither 34
    New pain 35
Part Three: Insomnia 36
    Conversation with Insomnia 37
    Disconnected 39
    Unwinding 40
    Rumi Speaks To Me 41
    Another Night 42
    Ginsberg Sheets 43
    Midnight Blue 44
    Gossiping Trumpet 45
    Night-Blooming Cereus 46
About The Author 51
Praise For *Insomnia* 52

ACKNOWLEDGMENTS

A special thank you to Daniel García Ordaz for helping me through the darkness. Love you my brother. Ileana García-Spitz for capturing me at my best and worst and still believing in me. To every artist who stays true to his or her art and contributes in making the Rio Grande Valley of South Texas a beautiful place to create and live.

Fragments of most of these writings were posted on facebook, therefore . . . Thank you, Facebook.

To the Muses that have inspired these writings, thank you!

To my brothers, Aldo & Albert: I love & miss you guys so much. During the sleepless hours I think of our growing up together and survival of living in the projects.

A ti, Madrecita. Gracias por tu amor, oraciones, paciencia y cariño.

Eloy, I love you, Viejo. Siempre te he querido como padre en mi vida.

EDWARD VIDAURRE

INTRODUCTION

**Bloodshot and Always Awake:
An Exploration of Voice, Influence, and Evolution
Katherine Hoerth**

I first met Edward Vidaurre at an open mic poetry reading back in 2011. He was new in our humble poetry scene, and I remember, as the evening was winding down, he took the mic. We were on the patio of this Cuban restaurant; my beer was empty and my belly was full like the midnight moon that hovered above us. Edward's words awoke me from my daze, demanded my attention, my wonder. He left the audience breathless, and from that moment on, the poetry scene in the Rio Grande Valley was changed.

Insomnia is steeped with this same energy, and though I've had the pleasure of witnessing his evolution as a poet, this vibrancy is constant. This is a collection of poems that make us celebrate the ennui, find holiness in the down-trodden moments of our lives, make us feel the magic of that mysterious crack between sleeping and waking, that illustrate the complexities of our daily lives both here in El Valle and beyond.

Edward's poetry, reminiscent of the Beats, explores the beauty and truth of being the common man. In poems such as "When the Soul Sleeps" we see references to Ginsberg, discovering "the mean truth" about life, that "we dream in tunnels / we, the down trodden." The poem continues:

> We listen to the howls
> Of the forgotten poets
> The ones who see
>
> The night
> Vomit into the sea.

INSOMNIA

Like the Beats, the speaker identifies with the existence of the down-trodden, incorporating sharp images of "a hobo smacking his lips / after a swig of rawness" or "falling leaves" that "feel like guillotines over the head of sugar mill workers in autumn." But it's a matter of finding holiness, of truth, not brokenness in these images. In "Ginsberg Sheets" the speaker, in a more direct manner, claims this heritage, describing a chillingly beautiful death by falling onto the pavement, "splattering poems, bleeding ink" with a toe tag that reads "UNKNOWN BEAT."

Insomnia also reminds me, as a reader, of the fantastic magical realism of Lorca, where mermaids witness the salty euphoria of two lovers and "swim away in tears" that "drown along with the moon that leaves its shadow on the wall," (22). It incorporates the fanciful and seemingly impossible leaps of Bly – where the world seems like a dream, "like a colt running from the devil morphing into a unicorn … gentle like the shy fog that blankets the resacas."

But above all, Edward's voice is his own. These poems are also regional, poems that masterfully illustrate the quirkiness of life in El Valle through the eyes of a Barrio Poet. Come down the resacas of the lower valley with Rumi and watch "the rocks under [your] feet dance" towards their drowning death in its waters. Dream of a "raspa-colored heaven" where the "skies are blue coconut and chamoy." Listen to the song of border-town barrios at night – a barking dog, an opening door, "a mother's heart" with her "mouth wide open / screaming into the dead night without a sound." These poems illustrate what life is like when you live with your eyes open, bloodshot and always awake.

Katherine Hoerth is the award-winning author of *Among The Mariposas* (Mouthfeel Press, 2010) and editor of *Twenty: In Memoriam*, among several book and journal publications. Her blog appears at http://katiehoerth.blogspot.com/.

EDWARD VIDAURRE

Part One: Night

"How did it get so late so soon?"
— Dr. Seuss

Sleep Apnea

It's that time of the night when apples and peaches taste different. When she's afraid to make eye contact and chemistry becomes dangerous. When your feet want to walk backwards and your knees bend inward, your hands sweat and your stomach wants to leave your body. When death comes and tattoos bags under your eyes as you struggle in your suspension of external breathing.

EDWARD VIDAURRE

Submerged

Let me finish this poem
before you disappear
into the India ink across
my chest.

I only dream of you
on nights when
the sullen fog drifts
into the broken wood bridge
near the resaca where
my body appeared to
the barefoot children
de mi colonia

Sirena sumergida,
las aguas lloran por ti
las aguas lloran por ti

Everything you do,
you do in secret,
you think in code,
and speak in murmurs
yet,
when you speak of love
it's loud and clear
for my heart
and that is enough
for me

that is enough for me

en tus ojos descanso,
en tus ojos descanso...
undido

INSOMNIA

The Well

The moon and my shadow are creepy conspirators.
They make promises with bread offerings
to the mountains and piss away
with laughter on the shores
that make lyrics for lovers.

They commit crimes,
get away with them
by hiding in the hearts of saints.

I wait for my shadow under lamp posts
and give up when the fireflies begin
to tease me. But, I will write
them both into a hole,
where they can hug in the dark—
neither one knowing

who belongs
to who or what.
Above them,
me and a boulder . . .

EDWARD VIDAURRE

Siesta Haikus

uno.

Curled up position
Hands holding an angel's face
Shadow sets alarm

dos.

Once upon a time,
Swinging, dodging, the sea mist
Hammock snapped in two

tres.

Disguised as a nap,
Dreams drink from my mind: one gulp
Two gulp, three gulp, four . . .

cuatro.

Baby drools and sleeps.
Outside her window, a sweet
Hummingbird flies off.

Resaca Dreams

This poem is accompanied
by a slow strumming guitar

sung by the many voices
lost in the prodigal whispers

of mort—the piety of the poor,
the cachinnation of border town

children, the wisdom of the viejitas
y viejitos, and, finally . . . by the moon

that painfully shines a light on my greatest
fear: a floating love that wished to be a mermaid

instead morphing into a catán.

Editor's note: a catán is an alligator gar—a large, toothy, freshwater fish

EDWARD VIDAURRE

Our First Song

A jazz tune, a song
Davis by the river, blue
entering my mind

INSOMNIA

Pantoum Dream

I will dream of ancient rains that fall
drop by drop
beat by beat
from the blood-red skies

drop by drop
from the faucet of humanity
from the blood-red skies
the souls of purgatory will cry

from the faucet of humanity
saints will wander,
the souls of purgatory will cry
lost in nostalgic dreams

saints will wander,
amongst the daydreamers,
lost in nostalgic dreams
breathing towards a vanishing afterlife

amongst the daydreamers,
side-by-side with forgotten lovers,
breathing towards a vanishing afterlife
my heart slows down

side-by-side with forgotten lovers,
poems become hymns and
my heart slows down
diminished

poems become hymns and
watch the lonely moon drown in the black waters below—
diminished,
forgotten and in love—
alone.

EDWARD VIDAURRE

At Your Front Door

You live out in the middle of nowhere. The doorbell rings. It's five past midnight. The dog pants and the oak tree out front brings its leaves to a hush. The cookie dips into the ice cream slowly. You try to quiet your breathing. There's a knock this time. The phone rings. Your heart stops. The door opens. The dog runs. You fade.

In A Brief Instance, She Vanished . . . Like A Whispered Kiss On The Fingertips

Like a northern wind disturbing
an afternoon siesta
      making me forget
the end of the dream

Like a peripheral vision
    of great grandma holding her
heart, strung to a star
        leaving drops of blood
for the stray cat to lick

Like a hobo smacking his lips
after a swig of rawness
      killing what's left of his dignity

Like pennies in a wishing well
      drowning a child trying to steal
its riches

Like the creepy fog that gossips from
town to town
      in search of
a wailing woman
      with bite marks
on her ankles.

EDWARD VIDAURRE

My Poetise Incognito

I come out at night
or when my shadow permits

sometimes, not at all

INSOMNIA

When The Soul Sleeps

I blame insomnia on artificial whispers.
See through the bitterness of winter.
There will be time later for weeping.

The trees translate our tears
as petty nurturing of their roots.
Everyone can see their ribs

broken. Like twenty-dollar
knock-off Rolex watches,
they tick instead of glide.

Lonely men keep their
heads hung low, trying
not to stare at the cliché

of grey skies
that haunt the floors
of heaven.

The mean truth is:
we dream in tunnels,
we, the downtrodden.

We listen to the howls
of the forgotten poets—
the ones who see

the night
vomit into the sea.
It is the salt that

tells us what it means
in songs that come ashore
when the soul sleeps.

EDWARD VIDAURRE

Absence of Light

She speaks in music, in lyrics. "There's a light that never goes out," she murmurs. I look and agree with her. It's true! No matter how tightly we close our eyes, there is a hint of light, sometimes in zig-zag threads that lick the outer layer of our eyes when shut. When I was a kid I enjoyed facing up to the bright sun with my eyes shut tightly and counted to thirty, then opened them up and scan the world around me. The universe would be on fire with oranges and reds until nature painted its canvas back to its appropriate shades. Today I would like to see everything in baby blue, the grass and trees, coffee and eggs. Why not? She bleeds and squirms in pain on her knees. Why can't the blood running between her thighs be in rainbows? Maybe in florescent pink? Sometimes I want total blackness, but the silver lines appear and escape behind a door that is not there. "There's a light that never goes out." I agree.

Just an absence.

INSOMNIA

Night

I'm writing in the dark.
The exhaled smoke makes creepy images
that dance into this bitch of a night.

I'm writing in the dark.
The mosquitoes line up.
I see them take flight towards me
as they die into this night.

This bitch night—
pale,
still—
hot mess of a night.

EDWARD VIDAURRE

I Lost My Soul In The River Styx That Flows From Between Your Thighs

I'll call that agony of space
Phlegethon,

where I will wade my hands
on the side of each tower
upward into the ecstasy
of your sheath.

I lost my soul
exploring the
passage of humanity,

plunging into
experience. Like Thetis,
be my mother and dip me
into the darkness of your
hungry river.

Are you Charon?
What or how much
do I owe you?

When will you swallow me?

Part Two: Morning

"Coffee, please. Black."

EDWARD VIDAURRE

Fragments

Last night I dreamed about you. You left your lips on my pillow and toes on the dresser, you left your shoes under the bed and your earrings in my mouth, you left your hands on my chest and thighs on the chair in the corner, you left your breath on my neck and ring in my hand. Your breasts are still on top of the radio, and your eyes . . .

    well, your eyes . . .

        I'm wearing them.

How Quickly The Leaves Razor Over The Heads Of The Mill Workers
(for Rodney Gómez)

I.

I dreamed of a girl from Lowell,
a sepia tone reverie
—her hair, dry as desert sand,
she walked out on her pots and pans
to pine away and die

II.

Fight! is what mattered
New Year's Day, one-nine-one-two
Cold day in Lawrence

III.

No one noticed her rosy cheeks and soft humming of a childhood song as she fitted her bonnet. It belonged to her late aunt, and like her late aunt she kept it neat and didn't mind that the euonymus etched on her skirt was foreign to her. She came for bread but demanded roses. Bajo el manto de la oscuridad cuidaba un secreto negro como la noche sin luna. Solita se fue caminando. No se supo mas de ella.

IV.

Falling leaves feel like guillotines over the head of the sugar mill workers in autumn.

EDWARD VIDAURRE

My Darling Son, My Warm Heart

My build-a-boy . . .
I dream of your tiny hands
and little man voice,

stare at you for hours—
especially when you sleep—
kiss your face
and tiny feet,

watch you play
with trucks and Lego blocks,
army men, marbles
—as a cop.

My darling son, my warm heart . . .
you've been gone for over a decade.
I never stopped counting.
There's still wreckage.

You were pulled from your mother
eight months premature.
I see your footprints up above,
on a cloud, on a star—yours, I'm sure.

    No choice—
    not for me—
    same day,
    my revenge
    took her to Disney.

INSOMNIA

Unrequited Love: A Sestina

He walks in a state of euphoria
Unnoticed—just watching—holding back tears,
her love, forbidden
his eyes see a mural on the wall
just over the bridge at the edge of the water
as she destroys his life with her thighs.

His kisses rise in between her thighs
as he wakes from a siesta filled with euphoria
that he can't shake until he splashes water
on his face to run down the drain along with his tears
resting against the bathroom wall.
Again he remembers she's forbidden,

her kiss remains forbidden,
and the fishnet stockings high up on her thighs
are lowered as she's pressed against the wall
wet with euphoria.
She smiles through her tears
at the sound of the crashing waves of water

under the bridge with his feet in the water.
His heart drops, forbidden
from loving her and kissing away her tears
that yearn for another to secure her thighs,
closely sending her into a euphoria
of emotions as she carves his name along with hers on the wall.

On the wall
with a mist of water
from the ocean's salty euphoria,
mermaids are forbidden
to watch and feel what he does between her thighs,
so they swim away in tears.

Their tears
drown along with the moon that leaves its shadow on the wall.
Her thighs,
pure as water,
killing the hearts of all men forbidden
from feeling her euphoria.

She drowns in the black water
as she waves at his name written in blood on the wall,
gasping away her euphoria.

INSOMNIA

The Recliner

She looks like she's been crying longer than it takes an oak tree to reach puberty. Long like a drought. Like starvation. She looks as if her face has been defeated by a three-year stint with insomnia. Her hair falls off like leaves in autumn that have been carried away by a river leading nowhere. Yet her beauty can't be denied. She will live long in the volumes of heroine fables told to children with a listening ear. Yesterday she made a rock feel like a baby chick in her hands, and it rolled around the caliche streets unafraid of being kicked around. It was the best day of its life. I sometimes dream that she stares outside her window just to see me pass by and that that look and all I see are her blinds dancing behind the fly-gutted screen that protects the window from dust and dirt particles in the summertime. I imagine she giggles and runs away like a child playing red light/green light before I can catch her. But then again, no. I imagine sometimes she walked away saddened that I wasn't the stormy-haired muchacho that makes her squirm and take long baths with the water running between her thighs. I make her the main focus in my dreams. There she spends the latter part of the day (when the sun is setting and the skies are a blue coconut and chamoy raspa-colored heaven) bent down, watering her plants and humming sweet songs in hopes they survive another Texas inferno. In my dreams she reads books about feminists, then sets them down and bakes cookies for the entire family. She doesn't see me in these dreams but smells the smoke of cherry tobacco coming from the recliner that has since been replaced by a large teddy bear with a rebozo tied around its neck. She lies on her back, rested. I dream that she will close her eyes and dream of me—strong, like a colt running from the devil and morphing into a unicorn with a platinum horn and golden wings, gentle like the shy fog that blankets the resacas that lullaby critters into a snooze. She eats me in her dreams, licks the hazel from my eyes and eats my fingers slowly. She wakes up full. I refill her day with spring water and organic vegetables. I invent new songs for her to hum to the herb plants. The dog barks at the recliner that sways on its own.

EDWARD VIDAURRE

Forgotten Man

If I slip away, will the mornings still greet you with dew drops on your front step? Will you see a book and think of me, or leave it to hide its treasure behind a candle that swallowed its wick to never glow again? Will the scent of me on your pillow that I take from you at night still linger, or will you replace it with a new set—less firm? If I slip away, will you call my name to the men wearing hats, with absurd beards, hoping they turn and smile? No one owns my face or voice. I will slip away into the pages of unread poetry books just squeezed in tight enough to become anthologies of the forgotten man—in libraries that hide us in corners where children aren't allowed—and alphabetically suffer.

Edible Earth

Today the earth is edible.
The mesquite looms
as if stuck in a yawn.
Go to it.
Take it apart and eat it.

The earth is edible.
The leaves are sweet.
The urinating caterpillar's
gift to you. Now go ahead,
drink from it.

It's tasty,
children! Run loose,
eat dirt, little loves.
The worms—chew them up
and laugh loud. Eat away
at your mother's rose garden,
thorns and all—bees and hummingbirds,
cats and dogs.

Let the homeless eat
the moldy walls of every
warehouse downtown. Your neighbor's
house too. Cardboard is protein man!

The earth is good!
for your soul, mind and body man!
Chew on dad's gun collection, corn cob pipe
his leather Lazy Boy and piled up newspapers.

Swallow smog, bite your cell phone,
grandma's sewing kit, pots and pans, wedding china.
Bite down on the passing train. Sink your teeth into
murals of black and brown heroes.

EDWARD VIDAURRE

Eat the grass if after all that good eatin'
Your tummy hurts.

INSOMNIA

Conversation With My Greñuda

What do I write for?

To make sense of how fast my daughter is growing
and how I'm slowing down.
She disappears into the blues, yellows, greens and tans
of the playground asking what the syringe on the floor is used for.

I tell her it's the sadness of what's left from last night's rain.
I tell her it's what's left of a fight between life and death.
I tell her
It's what's left.

She tells me
she thinks it's what keeps kids playing indoors,
building imaginary castles
and molding their future
with Play-Doh.

Though it makes no sense, she makes sense of it:
evil lurks, and if you're not right
wrong is magnified,
leading you to the edge between reason and insanity.

"Why is the playground empty?"
she asks.
I say it's because kids don't know how to play.

She says, "Or maybe parents need to be led by their hands
and not be afraid to get grass stains on their skinny jeans."
(There I knew she wasn't speaking about me.)
I say it may be true.
She says, "I'm glad you're my dad."
I say, "I'm glad you love swings and slides."

She smiles.

EDWARD VIDAURRE

How To Watch Me Wither

Sit on winter's lap.
Drink from the fountain of death.
Color the walls in mold.
Take a selfie at a funeral.

Sandbathe.
Yell obscenities at the moon.
Be fair and tell the sun its worth.

Drink tequila with a straw.
Read a poem to a mute parrot.
Grab a nopal by the throat.

Light up a cigarette from the wrong end.
Form a single-file line.

Point and shoot.

Lift me up again.
Don't give me water.

Inject me with sour milk
and hobo urine.

Take away my books,
and let me cry on the skin
of dead trees.

New Pain

I desire you
like South Texas—a new season.
Feel the wrap and execution

of my lips on yours.
Let it be painful,

like the pregnant moon
about to give birth

to a new earth.

Three: Insomnia

"The last refuge of the insomniac is a sense of superiority to the sleeping world."
— Leonard Cohen

Conversation with Insomnia

I like coffee. Dark nights with moonlit rays peeking through the window hoping to illuminate your body as you undress. I like kissing, and poetry, and sand between my toes, and cold beer. I like wine, jazz, great architecture, reading a beautiful woman's eyes. I like graffiti and the way new shoes feel. I like imperfect photography and soft porn late at night. I like laughing so hard depression sends tears through my eyes to remind me:
it's not
that funny.

I dreamt you again.

What was the dream?
I was kissing your fingertips—
you were crying—
and each time I kissed them, you cried more,
but they were good tears,
and they tasted like cotton—
whatever cotton tastes like— I just knew that it was the taste
of cotton.

Like cotton? . . . nice.
And then I searched for scars on your face,
and they were gone.
Your face was Photoshopped.
Your face tasted like baby's breath—
whatever baby's breath tastes like.
I kissed you everywhere but on the lips.

Why was that?
Not everywhere, but hands, arms, cheeks, eyes, neck,
and ears—like a mother cat does to her kittens.

Your hair kept getting in my face.

Tends to happen with the length of it.

EDWARD VIDAURRE

I was so close in my dream
I could taste you.
We shared each other's breath.

I like those kinds of dreams.
Yeah.
I suffer the most through them.

I believe you.
You spoke.
I listened,
but didn't hear.

In the dream?
Yes.
I cried.
I tried,
but couldn't,

so I died.

INSOMNIA

Disconnected

Lights out!
getting cold, quietness,
fridge is dead,
dark corners expand,
coffee cools,
poems lose shadow,
Christmas tree sighs,
the only noise

    —frustrating thoughts

EDWARD VIDAURRE

Unwinding

To my left
Erotic stories
To my right
A naked woman
In front of me
A poem with illustration

Rumi Speaks To Me

Wearing a red shirt,

the scent of empty garlic
and rotting peaches dance through
the window sills of my neighbors's homes.
When he visits, they never look out. They close their doors,
light candles, and hide in closets as the orchestra
of cacklin' bones comforts them.

The landlord says he wants to paint the walls blue.
I tell him that mold goes good with blue. He pauses and
understands.

Rumi agrees.

"Is it wrong for me to wish for poverty for myself?" "Is it selfish
for my family to do without?" Happiness is in the grappling of
bodies fighting for position against the sun, star gazing while the
moon has a jealous fit, listening to the requests of your daughter
wanting to go to the park to be pushed on the swing, reading a
book in silence, lying in bed watching a woman trace her lips with
the red that turns them from soft pillows on the face to an
explosion of Mujer?

Rumi is always fasting in my dreams.
No lentils. No bread.
He fills us both with music that makes the rocks
under our feet dance towards a resaca to their drowning death.
"This is necessary," he says, and I agree.

I ask, "When will I need to dance towards my death?"
The music stops. He disappears.
I am left with the scent of garlic and metal.

Rumi returns, with five things to say.
I listen, and I agree.

EDWARD VIDAURRE

Another Night

I shook in my sheets
the barrio stirred
dogs barked
doors opened
people spoke
the moon gave light
parents counted heads
two blocks down
one went uncounted
the news came fast
a mother's heart ached
she tore through the yellow tape
mouth wide open
screaming into the dead night
without a sound
another night
in my barrio
the silence is at times
too loud
too handle

sometimes

 at night

INSOMNIA

Ginsberg Sheets

Ginsberg sheets
soiled by the men
of a thousand kisses deep

Howling
for the Muses
to wake
to join in our insomnia

Restless nights
of blue midnight
sadness, waking up
to a somber jazz tune.
In the distance
where shadows have
lost their owners
to last night's suicide

I lie in Ginsberg's
sheets, soiled
by men with needle
tracks on their toes,
sitting next to windows,
looking out into
the third dimension
searching for zombie
hipsters in high-top sneakers.

I fall off,
counting the flights
until I reach your street,
splattering poems,
bleeding ink.

My toe tag reads:
UNKNOWN BEAT.

EDWARD VIDAURRE

Midnight Blue

If I played the harmonica, the sound would be of midnight blues, tattooed tears running down the face of God, of heroin blasts through unpainted canvases, a shrill of a deep shank into the breast of Mother Earth, the ripping from the roots of fruit trees being yanked from the concrete jungles of America's ghettos. If I played the harmonica—and played it well—the poor would hunger no more, and poetry would serve its purpose.

Gossiping Trumpet

I was about to speak
when rain fell.

When the shadows took over
and birds flew off,

the streets got cold and jazz
serenaded the drowning moon.

When I was able to speak again,
I knew that

the trailing tune of the
Gold trumpet stole my voice,

flew into the next town,
to gossip about our encounter.

EDWARD VIDAURRE

Night Blooming Cereus

I.

Time drops off,
like the petals
of a one-night stand

The evening lets
out a painful scream,
and just like that
you design the night
Like the cacti, long-
lasting for one moonlit
night, just long enough

—yet

too short to feel
the smoothness
and softness of the aromatic
memory of you
and sigh
of the coming fog

just like that
like the raging waves
of the big blue sea
wide open,
tumultuous

Then no more

II.

I tried to leave you, no denying it
Like the night-blooming cereus
You opened up

INSOMNIA

and closed the door of passion
before I could understand why
the bed was too narrow for
our bodies to clash

Yet, we did
Yet, there you went
short-lived

A sigh
I'll wake up to every morning
with petals by my feet,
the feel of your nipples
still imprinted on my lips

Once a year I die a little,
Once a year I live forever,

Once a year
I crave your lips
to ravish my doggish hunger

Once a year
I yearn
for your kill

III.

Flesh
Depth within my pangs
Of desire
I dwell in between
the soft, plush beat
-beat in my hands
fingers, tongue and lips

Flesh
Designed to drive a man

EDWARD VIDAURRE

To succumb to lust

I have no time to cherish
Your auburn hair, or listen
To your faint sighs

I'm comfortable and have
Little time before you fall apart
Like a cereus flower at dawn
Leaving the vein at attention
wanting a bit more

you drop
and scatter across the
plains of organic fields
leaving your scent trailing.

In the end
I fade and wait
For you to bloom again

Tomorrow night

Or maybe never

I'll take my chances
Until I can catch your fall from grace
Into my failing hands

IV.

the moon sang to you,
an ode, perhaps a whisper,
that perished by dawn

V.

I will kiss you until you
and I both   fall apart

INSOMNIA

until your moans
and my poetry become harmony,
until my fingertips make swirls
in the sky -matching your spiral drop,
until my sweat irrigates the landscape
that feeds your life,
until our orgasms stop time,
until one night   becomes
forever

EDWARD VIDAURRE

ABOUT THE AUTHOR

Conceived in El Salvador and born in Los Angeles, California, in 1973, Edward Vidaurre, has been published in several anthologies and literary journals, among them: *La Bloga, Bordersenses, Interstice, La Noria Literary Journal, Left Hand of the Father, Brooklyn & Boyle,* and *Boundless*—the Anthology of the Valley International Poetry Festival 2011, 2012, & 2013. His book *I Took My Barrio On A Road Trip* (Slough Press) was published in 2013.

Vidaurre co-edited *TWENTY: Poems in Memoriam*, an anthology in response to the Newtown, CT, tragedy, and *Boundless 2014*: the Anthology of the Rio Grande Valley International Poetry Festival.

His work has been nominated for the Pushcart Prize. He resides in Edinburg, Texas, with his wife and daughter.

He hasn't slept well in years.

EDWARD VIDAURRE

IN PRAISE OF *INSOMNIA*

Edward Vidaurre consistently amazes me with his ability to take the very simple, very common things he notices in his life, like a child's smile or just the right cup of coffee, and he uses them as a launch pad for poems that take us to the universal realm.

Vidaurre is a self-taught poet with eyes to see, a heart to feel, and a passion to keep sharing through shadows, confusion, and changes. His work always leaves me with a sense that I have learned new things about myself, though his words and insights are his alone.

PW Covington, author of *I Did Not Go Looking For This*

~*~

Pick up this book on those weird and wonderful nights when it's 2:07 a.m. and the waning echoes of yesterday's shattered dreams and sprightly nightmares reverberate madly against the thickly transparent rays of the unsympathetic moon. In this collection of poems, Edward Vidaurre captures the lingering accusations and celebrations of the night that mingle with the fresh affirmations of the morning through poems filled at times with umbrage and desperation and at others with the sort of devilish charm that has come to define his candid wit. Like a bad dream that won't go away or a good dream that just makes one's day, Vidaurre's new collection, *Insomnia*, rouses us with a twitchy, spilt-coffee jerk that stirs us with knowing nods into those moments of clarity and opaqueness, of sweetness and acrimony, of haunting realism that can't help but keep us awake to read just one more poem.

Daniel García Ordaz, author of *You Know What I'm Sayin'?*

The poetry of Edward Vidaurre overwhelms one with an insomnia so desperate yet so sweet. A barrio of love constantly surfaces just before he falls asleep and keeps him and us awake with raw truths. Those truths which most of us won't admit to. But the poet is left with no choice. Vidaurre's lyricism reminds one of Omar Salinas, but with a surrealism that bubbles full of reality.

> Poet Reyes Cárdenas, author of *Anti-Bicicleta Haiku* (1976), *Survivors of the Chicano Titanic* (1981), *Elegies For John Lennon* (1984, 2006), *I Was Never A Militant Chicano* (1986), and *Chicano Poet: 1970–2010* (2013)

~*~

Combining Lorca-like meditation with the boldness of Bukowski, Vidaurre blends stark imagery and his unique voice to emerge as a powerful new literary force . . .

> Joseph D. Haske, author of *North Dixie Highway*

~*~

In his latest collection of poetry, Edward Vidaurre explores every moonlit nook and cranny of the insomniac night—visions both nightmarish and beautiful, brought on by lack of sleep—and the coffee-fueled, bleary-eyed morning that comes close on its heels. The poems he discovers in the borderland between wakefulness and slumber are full of startling images, purgatories brimming with fingertips and thighs, rivers and blood, howls and laughter, ghosts and the afterimages of bright smiles. From formal to experimental, Vidaurre's irrepressible, unique voice echoes in verse . . . .

David Bowles, award-winning poet of *Flower, Song, Dance: Aztec and Mayan Poetry*

Made in the USA
Monee, IL
03 September 2023